Pumpkin Days

By Melissa Nicholas

Sadlier-Oxford
A Division of William H. Sadlier, Inc.

People grow pumpkins here.

People pick pumpkins here.

People weigh pumpkins here.

People pay for pumpkins here.

People put pumpkins here.

People put pumpkins there.

And some people put
pumpkin in a pie. Yum!